FEELING GREAT

How to change your life for the better

DADI JANKI

BRAHMA KUMARIS
WORLD SPIRITUAL UNIVERSITY · BKIS

Feeling Great
Dadi Janki

First Edition 2010

ISBN 978-1-886872-61-5

Published by Brahma Kumaris Information Services Ltd., in
association with Brahma Kumaris World Spiritual University (UK)
Registered Charity No. 269971.

Global Co-operation House, 65 Pound Lane, London NW10 2HH, UK

Copyright ©2010 Brahma Kumaris Information Services Ltd.

Compiled and edited by Anthony Strano

Designed by Sameer Patro
Printed by Wyndeham Grange Limited, UK

www.bkpublications.com
email: enquiries@bkpublications.com
www.bkwsu.org

This book has been written to commemorate Dadi Janki's 40 years of foreign service in the West and 75 years of world service

Foreword

Is it possible to feel great in today's world, where every day there seems to be some new crisis, or disorder? Some new upheaval or unexpected negativity? Where violence is so rife? Should we even strive to feel great? Maybe it's out of place, or insensitive to the realities of many people's lives?

This little guide draws on decades of spiritual study and experience. The author includes rich descriptions of the sticking points we may encounter in our journey through life, as well as setting out the keys to making progress, as we recover our ability to feel really great — not as a temporary indulgence but as a lasting state of being.

We learn, for example, about the 'gravity' of negativity, when 'clogged' emotions such as resentment, wounded pride and rejection hold us down and drain all goodwill and spontaneity from our lives.

Enthusiasm, optimism and contentment are among the keys that can free us from such chains. We learn that these qualities spring from faith in the goodness of the self and life. This faith returns to us when we start to understand the wonderful Tree of Humanity and the eternal Seed through which it is renewed.

In essence, love enables us to feel great. Love is in all of us, but in order to flourish, it needs to be tended with spirituality. When we demand love from the world around us, we destroy our ability to receive it.

The Brahma Kumaris World Spiritual University is a global community of people learning how to increase their ability to live with love. Readers new to the organisation can find out more at www.bkwsu.org, including a guide to the location of centres across the world.

Contents

How To Feel Great

Feeling great begins with inner harmony,
honesty, friendship and peace.

Harmony

Feeling great is about putting our life in order, rather than having a good time or feeling good at any cost. It is about bringing our inner world into harmony, developing the maturity to align our inner world of thoughts, attitudes and feelings with our outer world of actions, words and relationships. If there is confusion inside, there will be confusion outside.

Honesty

To begin to feel great we need to become more honest – to make what we think, say, feel and do as one. Without this "oneness" in our personal lives, no amount of distracting fun can make us feel good, positive or great.

Having honesty means taking responsibility for the way we think, feel and respond to situations and other people. We can start by addressing a few questions to the self:

- Did I really need to do that action?
- Did I need to think that?
- Could I have spoken, or acted, in a better way?

Questions like this clean out our bad habits and ordinary ways of living. We cannot feel great if we have bad habits.

One common bad habit is letting others throw their rubbish into our lives, either in obvious physical ways or more subtly. Why do we allow them to do this? "Because of this" or "because of that" perhaps – but 'because' statements only help us to justify our miserable feelings or the situation. How can we feel great when we are complaining or constantly pessimistic, fearful or in a state of suppressed anger? How can we feel great if we are not free to be the master our own life?

Freedom

Real freedom, begins with me. I cannot blame others for what they are doing to me. It is a waste of time to examine their actions repeatedly and become angry. I can only examine what I am doing to myself and ask "How long will I continue to live like this?"

Other people are actors in this unlimited Play of Life. They will do what they wish to do, and exist as they like — but I can choose in which direction to move. I decide whether or not to be influenced, compelled or used by others. To feel good, positive and/or great, I realise that I need to change. A better way of life is in my hands, not in the hands of others, whether they be spouse, child, boss, priest, guru, politician or doctor.

Friendship

One of the things that makes us feel great is friendship. Friendship is the basis of every genuine relationship. But it has to begin with me. Until I take responsibility for and start listening to myself, I cannot be my own friend. Am I kind and loving to myself? Are my thoughts, feelings, attitudes, words and actions friends with each other, or are they often in contradiction and out of control? Inner harmony and honesty begins the flow of friendship between me and the outside world —

not only the world of the other actors in my life but the worlds of time, nature and matter.

Creating this kind of partnership, in which I feel positively connected to all other aspects of life, creates a great feeling – for this is the feeling of fulfillment.

Inner Peace

Feeling great begins with stepping inside to meet our self; to observe how our inner world is functioning, what thoughts and feelings there are and how we are creating them.

When we step inside and see and accept our self as we are, we begin to create peace within. The original peace that is at the core of our being starts to flow. Positivity is the natural outcome of this experience of peace.

When the feeling of peace and positivity remains constant, no outside event or other person can interrupt the flow. However, to begin with the feeling of peace may ebb and flow and our feelings and mood fluctuate. This confuses us and those around us. They have to deal with our swings and imbalances and can never be quite sure how to position themselves when dealing with us. They certainly do not feel great.

Feeling great must encompass the capacity to remain stable in whatever positive attitude we have — and that makes others feel great.

The Keys To Feeling Great

Key of enthusiasm, key of optimism,
key of contentment.

The key of enthusiasm

Enthusiasm is the master key to feeling great. It acts like a double energy boost. It keeps the self extremely positive and beyond the pull of negativity while simultaneously making others feel uplifted too. It's as if enthusiasm opens a window, 'unsticking' other people from a narrow state of mind, gloom or despondency. Enthusiasm gives us faith in the reality of other possibilities.

The word 'enthusiasm' is derived from the Greek word *enthusiasmos*, meaning 'to be in God', or 'to be in the divine'. When we are spiritually alive and in tune we are able to see, think, feel and act in new and creative ways if faced with a 'blocked' situation.

For example, a person with enthusiasm never sees a problem as a 'problem', or an obstacle as an 'obstacle'. They are lifted above the pull of fear, doubt or pessimism. Instead they envisage solutions, create bridges and, rather than fighting an obstacle, simply dissolve it. Enthusiasm is a therapy that breaks the gravity of negativity and shifts the type of 'mind-stickiness' that seems to trap people in a particular perspective or attitude no matter how harmful it might be.

To develop enthusiasm, have faith in the goodness of life, and in the original goodness of the self and others. Believe that no matter what happens, no matter how sorrowful or incomprehensible something may appear to be, behind the dark curtain there lies a hidden lesson or an unforeseen benefit.

Such enthusiasm gives us strength and direction when our thoughts spiral out of control or spin in tiring circles. It is also great therapy for a wounded heart, when emotions such as resentment, hurt pride and rejection drain our goodwill and spontaneity.

Enthusiasm is such an important factor in feeling great that in India a goddess has been created to represent this creative, benevolent and uplifting energy. Uma is her name, and she is constantly invoked for well-being.

The key of optimism

Optimism opens a door in difficult or hopeless situations. Optimism knows that there is always a way, no matter how many doors have been shut. Optimism believes that there is always a useful alternative.

No matter what the crisis, an optimist maintains the outlook that it is a sign, time for a different way of thinking, or a new way of doing things. Sometimes the signal has to be very clear, even harsh, otherwise we may continue in self-delusion and not wake up. Of course, if we lack optimism, instead of taking this signal as a step towards renaissance, complaint, resentment or even desperation will emerge.

Optimists hold on to hope. They do not ignore the reality and consequences of negativity, but they do not despair or lose themselves in the chaos that ensues when Pandora's Box is opened, releasing into the world all things that are bad. There are many such boxes in daily life which are often opened but optimism enables us to find solutions to the problems that assault us.

Knowing that bridges can be built, seeing that after a storm rainbows shine their many colours, optimists never give up. They trust in life and work with patience and determination. It is clear to them that if they do give up, Pandora's Box will remain open and all kinds of demons – of fear, chaos and distress – will keep emerging.

To become an optimist maintain a gentle determination that allows you to focus on possible alternatives, and find solutions to problems. Be flexible and able to be led. Combine the art of making things happen with the ability to allow things to happen, knowing that it is all a matter of timing. Realise that more than one factor needs to be considered in order to successfully build a bridge or find a solution.

The key of contentment

Contentment lays the foundation for happiness. Happiness not only makes us feel great, but in the East is thought to be the best medicine because this state of being contains within it so much optimism and enthusiasm.

Contentment should not be confused with complacency. To be complacent is to achieve a state of subtle arrogance, thinking, "I have reached my goal. No need for anything further. I am fine," followed by the shutting down of both creativity and the willingness to bring about personal change.

To be content, appreciate where you have reached, value your efforts yet realise that there is more to learn and keep yourself open to that new learning.

Being content leads to a sense of progress, a feeling that, "I have found something very good, but let us make it better and ultimately the best."

Contentment comes from appreciation – from a deep gratitude for all the things life gives us and heartfelt thanks that God has given us the capacity to learn and exist meaningfully.

The father of contentment is humility, the openness to receiving new signals from life as well as the courage to act on them. The mother of contentment is simplicity because it is the simple things in life that create its wonder, such as breath, thought, choice, the sunlight, flowers and a smile.

Nothing is taken for granted when we know true contentment. We cherish and value everything. Because of this inner awareness we do not compare ourselves with others, or feel inferior or superior, but simply have the great feeling that everyone is good and everything is good.

Why We Stop
Feeling Great

There are many reasons why we lose our ability
to feel great, but at the core there are four bad
habits: forgetfulness, the game of substitute,
disconnection from God and busyness.

Forgetfulness

The most draining of the four habits is our ability to forget our original identity.

Losing awareness of the soul-self is a major reason why we feel empty, unhappy or cheated, humiliated, depressed or desperate and the rest of the long list of negatives we are so familiar with.

Forgetting who we are results in a total reliance on external achievements and social position as ways of evaluating the self. It creates a dependence on others and their opinions, and a need for constant approval.

Such identification with the social and physical self wipes out our awareness of the wondrous eternal blueprint of life that each of us is. I forget that I am a spiritual being; a soul.

In this forgetting of what we are, we also forget what others are, and the result of all this forgetting is a lack of respect on all levels. Instead of a culture of respect and acceptance, there is a growing global culture of disintegration and blame. Integration and respectfulness have largely disappeared. Although many people realise this and make a great deal of effort, both individually and collectively, to create respect and a culture of oneness, nevertheless selfishness dominates. This explains the great violence we are witnessing on so many levels of life today.

The antidote

In order to start returning to respect, return to an awareness and experience of your

original serene self, thinking about the tiny
point of spiritual energy deep within us
all will make you feel great. Thoughts and
feelings created from that original blueprint
can never be selfish, vicious or harmful.
Anger or conflict, hate or fear will stop
draining you and you will quite naturally
share your positivity with others.

The first and original power of that blueprint of
being is peace or, more aptly, serenity. Although
both express the basis of true human living i.e.
non-violence, serenity includes a feeling of
completeness and contentment. When we live
in this state of wholeness, no selfish needs can
trap us in the obligations, possessiveness or
attachments that cancel out any prospects of
feeling great.

The game of substitute (illusion)

When I am out of touch with myself, when I cannot relate to myself and others, a lack of connectedness follows, and this brings about a feeling of emptiness. I might try to fill this emptiness by clinging to others, to labels, to the glitter of the pseudo.

So much of advertising is based on the substitute game: if you eat this, wear these clothes or make-up, are seen here, then you will be regarded as fashionable, modern, acceptable and great. However, such illusions create extremely fragile images that can break easily when faced with a challenge or mishap. Too many 'castles in the air' are built throughout the globe on a materialistic code of values and an unscrupulous use of mass media combined with a lack of spiritual awareness. An abundance of false promises and dreams inspires 'copycat' lifestyles devoid of authenticity, which in turn promote a lack of connectedness to our roots.

When we lose our roots, we lose our child-like state. When we lose our innocence because of being influenced by the 'game of substitutes' promoted by the media, we cannot feel great. When we are deceived, we eventually experience the disappointment and wounds of living an unreflective life. The expression of 'substitute living' often takes the form of addiction and its consequence, depression, is now regarded as one of the world's most common diseases. Alternatively, a person may become bitter or cynical faced with such a loss of faith in goodness.

When such experiences occur, we may, either individually or collectively, decide to become defensive in order to protect the self. When we lack the courage and confidence to learn, self-defensiveness, based on fear, comes into play. Then how can we feel great?

When we substitute artificial things for real things, believing them to be real, there comes a great deal of pain.

For example, many people substitute 'attachment' for love and respect. Attachment creates the illusion of belonging when we identify with a particular person, position or group, we feel good. However, when those props disappear, for one reason or another, we are left bereft, lost, alone and desperate. We feel desolate.

Labels, no matter how socially acceptable, often become a substitute for real belonging. All people wish to belong to something or someone and do it through nationality, religion, social class, youth culture, fashion or a particular relationship. But this is only a substitute for the true belonging – to one's own self. This is the reality – because I am with myself all the time.

The antidote

Remain true to your original self and its qualities and values and artificiality will not be able to penetrate your truth.

Become both a child and a master as you journey along the spiritual path. As a child, remain open and trusting –and listen. As a master learn from experiences and realise their worth, no matter what the type of experience.

Learning and letting go of the past provide real protection for the self. When we inhabit a state of balance between master and child, we feel great. Great in the sense that nothing in life is irrelevant or a curse or a misfortune – everything has significance. Then, even if we face an enormous obstacle, we may not feel great but we will keep our sanity because when we trust, we know that life is for us, not against us. Disguised opportunities abound.

Disconnection from God

At this time in human history we seem to have lost our understanding and right connection with the Divine. No longer experiencing God as the gentle Father, the embracing Mother, the guiding Teacher and the loyal Friend, we do not feel safe in this universe. In fact we feel threatened and at the mercy of divine whim. We have lost confidence in Divine Love, which is as real as our own existence.

Consequently, we fail to trust in such a being, or we come across such wrong information that we prefer not to know or come too close. We are aware that religion has sometimes used the idea of God to aid human ambition and the desire to dominate, which is why there have been so many religious wars.

Furthermore, we know that some religious followers have been dogmatic and narrow-hearted, using their so-called relationship with God as a platform of superiority to justify inhumane behaviour.

Whether because of ritual, routines of worship or abstract concepts, God has become a distant figure for many people. Fear has replaced trust, judgment has replaced acceptance, and exclusiveness has replaced inclusiveness.

The antidote

Understand that the wonderful Tree of Humanity grows from the Eternal Seed of Life. Experience your connectedness. See everyone as your brothers and sisters. Become inclusive with all your heart and mind. Then you will feel great knowing that God is One and is for you and everyone. Through the One we, as a human family, will become one.

Busyness

Lastly we do not feel great because we often feel time is against us and not with us. The pressure to do rather than be is very great. The aim of life is to work hard in order to produce more and consume more. Time is squeezed by our stress. We push and shove to achieve anything and everything quickly without peace. We do not make the time to reflect and see our true intention and purpose. If our main value is greed and fear propels us to achieve, then time feels squeezed. We have 'no time to stand and stare' and we forget to stop and be quiet.

The antidote

Take seconds of quiet time during the day.
Master your thoughts and see clearly the
reasons why you do things. Examining your own
motives in this way will enable you to choose
a better course of action, or change direction
if your motives are not right or appropriate to
the situation. When you are no longer simply
dragged by the hair of need, desire or greed, you
will begin to feel great. You will have started to
master yourself and your life.

Ways To Start Feeling Great

Here are some practical methods to help us recognise and then overcome some of the habits or obstacles that stop us from feeling great.

Letting Go

We need to connect to and concentrate on the positive and the spiritual aspects of the self, making this the foundation of our change and learning. However, as realistic optimists, we must also be honest about the personal challenges and obstacles we must overcome if we are sincere in our wish to feel great and make others feel great.

In order to face and let go of a recurring block, or pain or sorrow, carefully practise the following five simple steps:

1. Recognise

Recognise that you have a recurring upheaval or problem. Admit to the self that something in you keeps coming back, irrespective of the person or situation that triggers the reaction. For example, you might feel unappreciated, misused and unable to find a co-operative person; you might have economic problems, or feel rejected or resentful. This is not about projecting blame onto others or situations. It is about recognising that everything, good or bad, begins with the self. This brings a great liberation because you know that you have all the inner resources to solve anything that has its roots in yourself.

Although you can seek co-operation from others, ultimately you have to do what needs to be done ourself. Acknowledge that the source of pain requires a change in your attitudes, thoughts and/or perception. When you take this responsibility you will stop feeling guilty and instead you will feel free to choose where you want to go and what direction your life will move in.

Honesty with the self never makes you feel guilty. Instead, it makes you feel great because, at last you have the courage to face yourself and you have the faith that by practising positive thoughts your world will change for the better.

2. Pinpoint

Pinpoint the flaw deep inside you while at the same time maintaining an awareness of the original blueprint of the self — that I, the soul, am those original qualities of peace, purity, love and happiness. In my original state I am free and balanced. I now just have to remember that state and return to it.

From the perspective of your original goodness will come a willingness and fearlessness that equips you to pinpoint clearly the flaw that has stopped you from feeling great.

3. Detach

After pinpointing the flaw, detach yourself from it. You can do this with confidence having the knowledge of your original true self. "I am not that flaw I see, I accept and I understand, but I do not identify with the object I am seeing, whatever it might be." This detachment creates a healing space, because, being honest, I do not become entangled in the flaw or feel unworthy, guilty or ashamed. Realising that the blockage has to go, I seek out the Surgeon who can operate on it. I wish to restore my spiritual and emotional health and feel great again.

4. Offer

Offer up your flaw to the Surgeon for an operation. As well as being our Father, Mother, Teacher and Friend, God is also the Surgeon who specialises in removing those things that make us feel bad.

He is a technically advanced surgeon, because He does not remove by cutting out but by dissolving. It is like leaving a piece of ice in the sun – it just dissolves. It is that easy. However, for such a dissolving to happen easily, you must make a profound decision. You must offer up the blockage and decide honestly that you do not want it any longer. For example the resentment that has lasted for years, the critical, judgmental nature that alienates so many, the constant fearfulness that cripples all initiatives.

Operations are not usually pleasant, but when we have an anaesthetic and trust in the surgeon they are not uncomfortable. The anaesthetic of divine love and trust in the Surgeon's skilled and gentle hand overcomes your hesitation. The operation done, you can move forward. There may be a little pain, in the form of fear, and old needs may re-emerge, but the operation has been successful even if some attention is still required.

5. Pay attention

Do not let any germs of old desires or fears come back and restart the process. Otherwise you will become infected and sick again. Since you wish to stay healthy, be careful and ask the Surgeon for advice on how to remain free and clean.

Having conquered all this, you feel great – your lost self-mastery has returned. You are no longer a victim or puppet of your old self, of others, or of circumstance.

The value of silence

The five steps that help us to start to feel well again require the quarantine of silence. The capacity for quietness – even the will for it – has been destroyed by an inner emptiness that demands to be filled with noise and emotions that, though superficial, keep emptiness at bay. A variety of noises and titillating emotions create the mirage of living and feeling great. The practice of silence educates us, helping us to understand what quietness is and its inestimable value in restoring the health both of our feelings and our thoughts.

Silence means unplugging, disconnecting from the many sockets that absorb our energy: problems, worry, pleasing, fear and overload. To be released quickly from all these debilitating socket points, we need to become introspective and quiet. This revitalise our thoughts.

Every thought we create is energy and it produces its own current, whether negative or positive. In quietness I step inside and connect to my original quality of peace, and I stabilise myself in the thought of that original peace. Then, slowly, I begin to feel great. This current of original peace releases me from burden and fear.

The power of Om Shanti

In meditation, the way to connect to our original peace is by using the thought 'Om Shanti.' The words signify the consciousness of our eternal state of peace and the awareness of our spiritual identity — they tell us that "I am a soul and a peaceful one." When I accept Om Shanti as a personal reality and concentrate upon it, the original power of peace and serenity is released. It is like new oxygen entering my mind. It feels great to have such a tranquil mind.

It takes just a few seconds of concentration to connect with the soul-self and release this current of upliftment. It can be practised a number of times during the day and only for about 10 to 20 seconds each time. This begins not only a good relationship with my mind but also a good relationship with time.

After a daily exercise of this practice, who can have any complaints about time? Who can make the excuse that "I never have time to practise seconds of silence"? Or say "It is impossible to be peaceful at work"? With this exercise there is always time to reconnect and recharge.

The *Om Shanti* current never fails to energise. However, we need to practise it with complete attentiveness. So, after a day of activity, having experienced many pauses of a few seconds of silence, we will not feel tired and we will still feel great.

The Principles of Feeling Great

Connecting with the Divine, Spiritual gardening, learning respect.

1. Connecting with the Divine

In silence, as I step back, I can observe my intentions, motives and responses to other people and situations. In order to improve a response and how I relate to others and events, I need the discernment to see both what I am doing and what needs to be changed.

Silence, the inner quietness, helps me to discern accurately. Without proper discernment and a decision to do things differently, I remain stuck in the rut of circular movement. The same things happen, the same things repeat. I feel frustrated and become both angry and hopeless and remain in the same position for years.

Silence and the discernment it brings with it move me upwards and forwards. In the heart of silence I find myself and I find God. He is

my partner in transformation. In the silence
I receive courage from Him and that inspires
me to move forwards. If I maintain the courage
to pioneer new movements in my life, His
response is unlimited. In India it is said, "When
I take one step of courage, God takes a thousand
steps towards me."

I feel great knowing that I am not judged
and labelled 'weak' or 'lazy', a 'no-hoper' or
'strange'. God's faith in me enables me to have
faith in myself. When I see myself through God's
eyes, I see my future as very bright, my present
as the most valuable opportunity, and my past
as my greatest learning. From the viewpoint
of eternity all is as it should be. There are no
regrets, only the inspiration to change for the
better - my potential is unlimited.

To have someone believe in me like this makes me feel not only great, but also supremely grateful that such pure feelings can come from another being to me.

This selfless embrace gives us the power to embrace the self and, especially, others. Then we simply do not see their weaknesses. We feel that any defect is curable and that any obstacle is simply a rung in the ladder upwards.

It is all a game. As long as we know a few of the basic rules, any of us can win. No degree is required, no particular social status, no nationality or religion — just an honest heart that blooms under God's light. This God-given opportunity can make anyone feel great.

2. Spiritual gardening

Knowledge is the seed, awareness is the earth, water is attentiveness and the light is God's benevolent co-operation. With this method of cultivation, the plant of understanding grows and the flower of virtue spreads its fragrance to all. Then, if an especially powerful fruit emerges, it is given to others – this a fruit that nourishes not only the self but many other people. Such spiritual gardening is a great joy. There is no better feeling than watching the self plant seeds of knowledge in the self. Through careful cultivation the self blooms and offers the fruit of achievements to others.

Whether we look on life as a game or spiritual gardening, certain principles must be understood and adhered to if we want good results. If the principles that govern life are understood and followed, there will be victory; there will be fruit. For example, if I plant watermelon seeds in winter, they will not grow because it is the wrong season to plant them. If I plant them in sand near the sea, they will not grow even if it is the right season because the earth is not right for them.

In a game each player has a position. If the referee grabs the ball and runs with it, the game is disrupted because that was not his role. If a player pushes another deliberately, he is disqualified because that is not the way to win.

The universe has principles, too, that maintain and sustain the right to well-being of all things: human souls, human bodies, animals, plants, water or earth. If we, as actors on the stage of life, do not stick to the principles that protect the right of all things to express themselves, disorder, chaos and crisis will follow. These consequences are not sent by God, they occur because human beings do not use their freedom responsibly. Breaking rules because of selfishness and not caring about the consequences of our actions causes upheaval on many levels. How can we feel great if we break the principles that maintain well-being?

3. Learning respect

The main universal principle is respect, from which comes acceptance, tolerance, inclusiveness and, ultimately, love. There are many steps to genuine love. Love is the power of the universe and it is God's nature. It is also the basic spiritual instinct of the human spirit, but it cannot be reached without the steps mentioned earlier.

The law of karma is the law of respect that maintains balance, order and harmony in the universe. When this law is broken, crisis will ensue. When nature and human hearts and minds are in upheaval, and violence is used so often to suppress, no one can feel good, positive or great. Those who use such disrespectful means to enforce their ideas and desires can never achieve lasting success.

Anything violent and disrespectful of an other's right to be is doomed to failure. Such ignorance is called Hell. Hell is when there is no peace and no respect, and brute force is regarded as almighty. When basic rights and basic goodwill are overturned by fear and greed, peace is lost.

Greed destroys all sense of security because what is gained is never enough – the religion of "More and More and More" rings throughout the cultures that live it. And this "more" is grabbed without any care of what happens to others. The fact that others become less or have less is ignored and justified by the slogan "survival of the fittest". Brutal selfishness decimating the forests, polluting the sky, throwing chemicals into rivers, seas and abusing humans brings its backlash in time. These crises awaken us to the fact that all life is precious and we need to get back on track. Many people are seeing and feeling this and there is a growing realisation that only the roots of our inherent spirituality can provide the basis for an authentic life.

A return to the Seed, to the original self and to universal principles can only enhance our existence. Because truth, progress or achievement mean that all feel great. Each person and form of nature feel the harmony of mutual belonging on this planet. In silence we can cultivate the seeds of knowledge and bring back the Garden of Eden. Hell, or Heaven, is on the Earth — it is up to us which we decide to create.

Feeling Great Now

This special time, a time for angels,

the way forward.

1. This special time

Time is one of our greatest assets and, especially now. God and time are offering us the opportunity to become anything we wish to be. Now seems to be a time of extremes: a great negative force is reaching its peak, but nonetheless, another greater positive force is also reaching its peak. We are in the middle of all this, and if we do not remain connected to our soul-self and the Supreme Source, it is very easy to become confused and even frightened.

Look closely, and you will realise that a cleansing process is taking place. All things – both in nature and in humanity – are returning to their original state of purity. In the process, many other negative things are emerging to be thrown out. Despite the explosions of negativity, the underlying current is one of renewal and renaissance. The false, iron time is being transformed into a time of golden truth: a culture of complete non-violence.

Using spiritual knowledge about the soul, God and of the principles of action will transform the chaos into harmony, strife into peace and selfishness into love. Although this transformation may not always be apparent, a positive turning towards peace and balance is quietly taking place.

2. A time for angels

Silence, knowledge and love are cocooning souls and in that silent depth a metamorphosis is taking place. Angels are being created on this planet, Earth. Human beings can and do become angels when they have a deep commitment to change and to serve.

These angels are not distracted by the scenes of violence, or by mastering and conquering their own selfish desires; they turn into light and become universal lighthouses guiding all to the eternal Home of Light – to the Father and Friend and the reality of the golden culture that is being created now. They feel great. In fact anyone who feels this great has discovered not only their own destiny, but also the great destiny of humanity.

3. The way forward

Every day we can build a better road to walk along. Every day we can make our own journey into the Light and fill ourselves. Every day we can make little changes that at some point will become a leap into a higher consciousness – the consciousness of oneness and belonging.

From this perspective, we see each other as equal, with the same right to inherit happiness and peace. When we know that all will receive their inheritance in their own way, at their own time, we feel great. In a family, all members wish each other well and help each other to receive the best that there is.

As the cycle of time finishes and the curtains of the theatre close and preparations are made for a new performance, there is great optimism. We feel great!

*"To feel good, positive and great,
I must realise that I need to change —
because a better way of life
is in my hands."*

Dadi Janki

WORLD HEADQUARTERS
PO Box No 2, Mount Abu 307501, Rajasthan, India
Tel: (+91) 2974 - 238261 to 68, Fax: (+91) 2974 - 238883
E-mail: abu@bkivv.org

INTERNATIONAL CO-ORDINATING OFFICE
& REGIONAL OFFICE FOR EUROPE AND THE MIDDLE EAST
Global Co-operation House, 65-69 Pound Lane,
London, NW10 2HH, UK
Tel: (+44) 208 727 3350, Fax: (+44) 208 727 3351
E-mail: london@bkwsu.org

AFRICA
Global Museum for a Better World, Maua Close, of Parklands
Road, Westlands, PO Box 123, Sarit Centre, Nairobi, Kenya
Tel: (+254) 20-374 3572, Fax: (+254) 20-374 3885
E-mail: nairobi@bkwsu.org

AUSTRALIA AND SOUTH EAST ASIA
78 Alt Street, Ashfield, Sydney, NSW 2131, Australia
Tel: (+61) 2 9716 7066, Fax: (+61) 2 9716 7795
E-mail: ashfeld@au.bkwsu.org

THE AMERICAS AND THE CARIBBEAN
Global Harmony House, 46 S. Middle Neck Road Great Neck,
NY 11021, USA
Tel: (+1) 516 773 0971, Fax: (+1) 516 773 0976
E-mail: newyork@bkwsu.org

RUSSIA, CIS AND THE BALTIC COUNTRIES
2 Gospitalnaya Ploschad, build. 1, Moscow - 111020, Russia
Tel: (+7) 495 263 02 47, Fax: (+7) 495 261 32 24
E-mail: moscow@bkwsu.org

Brahma Kumaris Publications
www.bkpublications.com
E-mail: enquiries@bkpublications.com

Brahma Kumaris World Spiritual University

The Brahma Kumaris World Spiritual University is an international organisation working at all levels of society for positive change. Established in 1937, the University now has more than 8,500 centres in over 100 countries.

Acknowledging the intrinsic worth and goodness of the inner self, the University teaches a practical method of meditation that helps people to cultivate their inner strengths and values.

The University has local centres around the world offering courses and seminars that encourage spirituality in daily life and cover topics such as positive thinking, anger management, stress relief and self esteem, amongst others. This spiritual approach is also brought into healthcare, social work, education, prisons and other community settings.

The University's Academy in Mount Abu, Rajasthan, India, offers individuals from all backgrounds a variety of life-long learning opportunities to help them recognise their inherent qualities and abilities in order to make the most of their lives.

The University also supports the Global Hospital and Research Centre in Mount Abu.

All courses and activities are offered free of charge.

www.bkwsu.org, www.bkwsu.org/uk